ExamREVIEW.NET

This book is available in PRINTED format only. If you are viewing a "downloadable" copy, the entity that provides you with the copy is in direction violation of the Federal Copyright Law and may be prosecuted. **Please be aware that our practice questions are NOT "realistic questions" or "past exam questions". We do NOT provide questions for cheating purpose!**

Intellectual Properties, Trademarks and Copyrights

ExamREVIEW.NET (a.k.a. ExamREVIEW) is an independent content developer not associated/affiliated with the certification vendor(s) mentioned throughout this book. The name(s), title(s) and award(s) of the certification exam(s) mentioned in this book are the trademark(s) of the respective certification vendor(s). We mention these name(s) and/or the relevant terminologies only for describing the relevant exam process(es) and knowledge.

We are vendor neutral. We are not affiliated with the relevant exam authority.

ExamREVIEW(TM) and ExamFOCUS(TM) are our own trademarks for publishing and marketing self-developed examprep books worldwide. The EXAMREVIEW.NET web site has been created on the Internet since January 2001. The EXAMFOCUS.NET division has its web presence established since 2009.

Contents of this book are fully copyrighted.

We develop study material entirely on our own. Braindump is strictly prohibited. This book comes with LIFE TIME FREE UPDATES. When you find a newer version, all you need to do is to go and download. **Please check our web site's Free Updates section regularly:**

http://www.examreview.net/free_updates.htm

Exam topics

The Certified Healthcare CPD Professional (CHCP) credential provides an educational self-assessment experience to those within the healthcare continuing professional development community and defines a standard of minimal competence for the healthcare education profession. The exam focuses on adult and interprofessional learning principles; educational activity planning, development, implementation, and evaluation; program leadership administration, and management; and knowledge of the CPD/CME/CE environment.

We create these self-practice test questions module referencing the concepts and principles currently valid in the exam. Each question comes with an answer and a short explanation which aids you in seeking further study information. Think of these as challenges presented to you so to assess your comprehension of the subject matters. The goal is to reinforce learning, to validate successful transference of knowledge and to identify areas of weakness that require remediation. The questions are NOT designed to "simulate" actual exam questions. "realistic" or actual questions that are for cheating purpose are not available in any of our products.

Throughout this book the "standard" refers to the ACCME standard.

Which standard ensures that accredited continuing education is free from commercial bias and marketing?

A. Standard #1

B. Standard #2

C. Standard #3

D. Standard #4

Answer: B. Standard #2

Explanation: Standard #2 focuses on preventing commercial bias and marketing in accredited continuing education.

Question 1

What is the primary goal of Standard #1 in the ACCME Standards for Integrity and Independence?

A. To manage commercial support appropriately

B. To ensure content is valid and supports safe, effective patient care

C. To disclose relevant financial relationships

D. To engage patients and public in CME

Answer: B. To ensure content is valid and supports safe, effective patient care

Explanation: Standard #1 aims to ensure that the education presented is fair, balanced, and supports safe, effective patient care.

Question 2

Which standard mandates the disclosure of financial relationships to ensure they do not influence accredited continuing education?

A. Standard #1

B. Standard #2

C. Standard #3

D. Standard #4

Answer: C. Standard #3

Explanation: Standard #3 requires identifying, mitigating, and disclosing relevant financial relationships to avoid influencing education.

Question 3

Standard #4 is primarily concerned with which aspect of accredited continuing education?

A. Ensuring content validity

B. Preventing commercial bias

C. Managing commercial support

D. Engaging interprofessional teams

Answer: C. Managing commercial support

Explanation: Standard #4 deals with managing commercial support to ensure education remains independent and free from commercial influence.

Question 4

Which type of organization is ineligible for ACCME accreditation?

A. Organizations providing clinical services directly to patients

B. Organizations marketing healthcare products

C. Organizations educating healthcare professionals

D. Organizations serving as fiduciaries to the public

Answer: B. Organizations marketing healthcare products

Explanation: Organizations primarily involved in producing, marketing, selling, or distributing healthcare products are ineligible for ACCME accreditation.

Question 5

What must be included in a provider's CME mission statement according to the Core Accreditation Criteria?

A. A list of educational activities

B. Expected results articulated in terms of changes in competence, performance, or patient outcomes

C. Financial disclosure information

D. Names of faculty members

Answer: B. Expected results articulated in terms of changes in competence, performance, or patient outcomes

Explanation: The CME mission statement must include expected results related to changes in competence, performance, or patient outcomes.

Question 6

How often must providers review enduring materials to ensure content validity?

A. Every year

B. Every two years

C. Every three years

D. Every five years

Answer: C. Every three years

Explanation: Providers must review enduring materials at least once every three years to ensure they remain up-to-date and accurate.

Question 7

What is the ACCME's requirement for attendance record retention for CME activities?

A. One year

B. Three years

C. Six years

D. Ten years

Answer: C. Six years

Explanation: Accredited providers must record and verify participation for six years from the date of the CME activity.

Question 8

What is meant by "professional practice gap" in the context of the Educational Needs Criterion?

A. A gap in funding for CME activities

B. A gap in knowledge among healthcare professionals

C. A gap between observed and achievable healthcare outcomes based on current knowledge

D. A gap in technology use in medical practice

Answer: C. A gap between observed and achievable healthcare outcomes based on current knowledge

Explanation: A professional practice gap refers to the difference between actual healthcare processes or outcomes and those potentially achievable based on current professional knowledge.

Question 9

How should accredited providers handle commercial support to ensure independence in education?

A. Accept all forms of support without restrictions

B. Allow commercial entities to influence content

C. Ensure that support does not result in commercial bias or influence

D. Disclose support only to internal stakeholders

Answer: C. Ensure that support does not result in commercial bias or influence

Explanation: Providers must manage commercial support to maintain the independence and integrity of the educational content.

Question 10

Which criterion focuses on the provider's ability to identify and implement changes in their overall program?

A. Educational Needs

B. Program Analysis

C. Program Improvements

D. Appropriate Formats

Answer: C. Program Improvements

Explanation: Program Improvements criterion involves identifying, planning, and implementing necessary changes to enhance the provider's ability to meet the CME mission.

Question 11

What does the criterion "Designed to Change" refer to in the context of CME activities?

A. Changing faculty members frequently

B. Generating activities that change competence, performance, or patient outcomes

C. Modifying the venue of CME activities

D. Updating financial disclosure policies

Answer: B. Generating activities that change competence, performance, or patient outcomes

Explanation: "Designed to Change" means creating educational interventions aimed at improving competence, performance, or patient outcomes as outlined in the mission statement.

Question 12

According to ACCME standards, who can serve as faculty for CME activities?

A. Only physicians

B. Only healthcare administrators

C. Both physicians and nonphysicians

D. Only board-certified specialists

Answer: C. Both physicians and nonphysicians

Explanation: Nonphysicians can also serve as faculty for CME activities.

Question 13

What must be included in educational formats chosen for CME activities?

A. Objectives and desired results of the activity

B. Financial information about the provider

C. Personal information of participants

D. Marketing materials from sponsors

Answer: A. Objectives and desired results of the activity

Explanation: Educational formats must align with the setting, objectives, and desired outcomes of the CME activity.

Question 14

How should accredited providers handle marketing by ineligible companies in conjunction with accredited continuing education?

A. Allow unrestricted marketing during CME activities

B. Separate marketing from the educational content

C. Incorporate marketing into the educational materials

D. Ignore the presence of marketing altogether

Answer: B. Separate marketing from the educational content

Explanation: Providers must ensure that marketing by ineligible companies is clearly separated from the accredited educational content.

Question 15

What is the requirement for analyzing changes in learners as a result of CME activities?

A. No analysis is needed

B. Analyze changes in competence, performance, or patient outcomes

C. Only analyze financial outcomes

D. Focus on attendance numbers only

Answer: B. Analyze changes in competence, performance, or patient outcomes

Explanation: Providers must analyze how their CME activities impact learners' competence, performance, or patient outcomes.

Question 16

Which criterion emphasizes the engagement of interprofessional teams in CME?

A. Designed to Change

B. Engages Teams

C. Program Analysis

D. Educational Needs

Answer: B. Engages Teams

Explanation: The Engages Teams criterion focuses on involving interprofessional teams in planning and delivering CME.

What must providers do to support the continuous professional development (CPD) of their CME team?

A. Only offer internal training sessions

B. Provide resources and opportunities for external learning

C. Exclude team members from CPD activities

D. Focus on financial incentives only

Answer: B. Provide resources and opportunities for external learning

Explanation: Providers should support CPD by offering resources and opportunities for learning beyond internal training sessions.

Question 18

What is required for providers who wish to apply for ACCME accreditation and are located outside the US?

A. They must partner with a US-based provider

B. They must attend an ACCME Accreditation Workshop

C. They need to translate their materials into English

D. They should limit their applications to online programs

Answer: B. They must attend an ACCME Accreditation Workshop

Explanation: Non-US based organizations must participate in an ACCME Accreditation Workshop as part of the application process.

What is the definition of "interprofessional team" according to the Engages Teams criterion?

A. A team composed exclusively of physicians

B. A team from multiple healthcare professions collaborating for better outcomes

C. A group of administrative staff planning CME activities

D. A committee of financial advisors overseeing CME budgets

Answer: B. A team from multiple healthcare professions collaborating for better outcomes

Explanation: An interprofessional team includes members from different healthcare professions working together to improve health outcomes.

Question 20

Why is it important to ensure content validity in CME activities?

A. To increase attendance rates

B. To meet accreditation requirements

C. To support safe, effective patient care

D. To secure commercial sponsorships

Answer: C. To support safe, effective patient care

Explanation: Ensuring content validity helps ensure that the education provided supports safe and effective patient care.

What does Standard #5 require regarding ancillary activities offered in conjunction with accredited CME?

A. They must be integrated into the CME content

B. They must be clearly separated from accredited CME

C. They should be marketed aggressively

D. They can include nonaccredited education without restrictions

Answer: B. They must be clearly separated from accredited CME

Explanation: Standard #5 ensures that ancillary activities, such as marketing or nonaccredited education, are kept separate from the accredited CME content.

Question 22

What type of data should providers use to advance healthcare improvement according to the Advances Data Use criterion?

A. Financial data only

B. Health and practice data

C. Marketing data

D. Attendance data

Answer: B. Health and practice data

Explanation: Providers should use health and practice data to identify areas for healthcare improvement and inform their CME activities.

Question 23

Which standard ensures that accredited continuing education is independent of commercial influence?

A. Standard #1

B. Standard #2

C. Standard #4

D. Standard #5

Answer: C. Standard #4

Explanation: Standard #4 ensures that education remains independent of commercial influence when commercial support is accepted.

Question 24

What action is required if educational material from a live activity is turned into an enduring material?

A. No action is required

B. Consider it a separate activity

C. Disclose it to ACCME

D. Combine it with the live activity records

Answer: B. Consider it a separate activity

Explanation: If live activity material is turned into an enduring material, it must be treated as a separate activity for ACCME purposes.

How long must activity documentation be retained for ACCME accreditation purposes?

A. One year

B. Three years

C. Current accreditation term or last twelve months

D. Ten years

Answer: C. Current accreditation term or last twelve months

Explanation: Activity documentation must be retained for the current accreditation term or the last twelve months, whichever is longer.

Question 26

Which type of support strategies are providers encouraged to use to enhance change in learners?

A. Financial incentives

B. Support strategies as an adjunct to CME

C. Mandatory participation

D. Public recognition programs

Answer: B. Support strategies as an adjunct to CME

Explanation: Providers should use support strategies, such as follow-up activities or tools, to reinforce learning and facilitate change.

Why must accredited providers ensure the separation of education from marketing by ineligible companies?

A. To increase attendance at CME activities

B. To comply with Standard #5

C. To reduce the cost of CME activities

D. To ensure marketing messages are included in educational content

Answer: B. To comply with Standard #5

Explanation: Standard #5 requires providers to maintain a clear separation between education and marketing to preserve the integrity of the CME content.

Question 28

What is the purpose of including the accreditation statement in CME promotional materials?

A. To attract more participants

B. To provide information about the educational content

C. To indicate the accreditation status of the provider

D. To highlight financial sponsors

Answer: C. To indicate the accreditation status of the provider

Explanation: The accreditation statement indicates that the provider is accredited and the activity meets ACCME standards.

Question 29

What role do patient/public representatives play in the planning and delivery of CME according to the Engages Patients/Public criterion?

A. They review financial records

B. They evaluate marketing strategies

C. They contribute to the planning and delivery of educational content

D. They recruit participants

Answer: C. They contribute to the planning and delivery of educational content

Explanation: Engaging patients/public representatives in planning and delivery helps ensure the education addresses relevant patient care and public health issues.

What must providers do to optimize communication skills in CME activities?

A. Focus on technical skills only

B. Include communication skill development as part of CME

C. Limit interaction among participants

D. Emphasize financial aspects of healthcare

Answer: B. Include communication skill development as part of CME

Explanation: Providers should design CME activities that help learners improve their communication skills for better patient interactions and outcomes.

What does the Creates Individualized Learning Plans criterion require from CME providers?

A. To create one-size-fits-all programs

B. To develop personalized learning plans for each learner

C. To focus only on group learning activities

D. To reduce the diversity of educational formats

Answer: B. To develop personalized learning plans for each learner

Explanation: This criterion requires providers to tailor learning plans to meet the individual needs of each learner.

What is one of the core responsibilities of accredited providers regarding the retention of activity and attendance records?

A. To keep records indefinitely

B. To retain records for six years

C. To destroy records after one year

D. To maintain records only for internal use

Answer: B. To retain records for six years

Explanation: Accredited providers must keep activity and attendance records for six years from the date of the CME activity.

Question 33

How should accredited providers handle the identification and implementation of program improvements?

A. Ignore feedback from learners

B. Plan and implement changes to improve the CME program based on identified needs

C. Focus solely on increasing financial support

D. Maintain the status quo regardless of feedback

Answer: B. Plan and implement changes to improve the CME program based on identified needs

Explanation: Providers must identify, plan, and implement necessary changes to enhance their ability to meet their CME mission.

Question 34

Which ACCME standard ensures that accredited continuing education is fair and balanced?

A. Standard #1

B. Standard #2

C. Standard #3

D. Standard #5

Answer: A. Standard #1

Explanation: Standard #1 ensures that the content of accredited continuing education is valid, fair, and balanced, supporting safe, effective patient care.

What is considered "healthcare quality improvement" in the Improves Healthcare Quality Criterion?

A. Improvements in clinical care processes or systems

B. Improvements in billing processes

C. Improvements in marketing strategies

D. Improvements in staff vacation policies

Answer: A Improvements in clinical care processes or systems

Explanation: Healthcare quality improvement refers specifically to enhancements in clinical care processes or systems, aiming to improve patient outcomes and healthcare delivery.

Question 36

For the Engages Patient Criterion, do patients and/or their family members who are involved in the planning and delivery of CME activities need to disclose all relevant financial relationships with any ACCME-defined commercial interest to the provider?

A. No, they are exempt from this requirement

B. Yes, they need to disclose all relevant financial relationships

C. Only if they request to do so

D. Only if they have financial relationships with more than one company

Answer: B Yes, they need to disclose all relevant financial relationships

Explanation: Patients and/or their family members must disclose all relevant financial relationships to ensure transparency and avoid any potential conflicts of interest in CME activities.

Question 37

What is the due date for submitting participant data for MOC activities?

A. December 31 of the reporting year

B. March 31 two years after the reporting year

C. December 31 the year after the reporting year

D. March 31 of the reporting year

Answer: B March 31 two years after the reporting year

Explanation: PARS will accept late learner completion data through March 31 two years after the reporting year, ensuring providers have ample time to submit necessary information.

Question 38

What is CME Passport and how can it benefit my physician learners?

A. A tool for tracking patient outcomes

B. A free search engine and web application for CME activities

C. A system for billing and insurance purposes

D. A certification program for medical educators

Answer: B   A free search engine and web application for CME activities

Explanation: CME Passport is a free, centralized web application where physicians can search for CME activities, track their progress, and generate transcripts of their CME and MOC/CC credits.

Can individuals disclose financial information to a provider verbally?

A. No, it must be in written form

B. Yes, verbal disclosure is acceptable

C. Only if they provide a notarized statement later

D. Only during certain approved meetings

Answer: B   Yes, verbal disclosure is acceptable

Explanation: Providers can accept verbal disclosure of financial information as long as they can verify and document it according to ACCME standards.

Question 40

Does the ACCME require a signed disclosure form to demonstrate compliance with Standard 3?

A. Yes, a signed form is mandatory

B. No, other methods of disclosure are acceptable

C. Only for certain high-risk activities

D. Only for faculty members

Answer: B   No, other methods of disclosure are acceptable

Explanation: The ACCME does not mandate a signed disclosure form; providers can collect disclosure information verbally, electronically, or through other documented methods.

Question 41

What is the ACCME's definition of an ineligible company?

A. Companies involved in medical research only

B. Companies providing clinical services

C. Companies offering healthcare education

D. Companies primarily producing or selling healthcare products

Answer: D   Companies primarily producing or selling healthcare products

Explanation: Ineligible companies are those primarily involved in producing, marketing, selling, reselling, or distributing healthcare products used by or on patients.

Question 42

What does "competence" refer to in the context of evaluating CME activities in the ACCME System?

A. The ability to recall facts

B. The extent to which learners implement what they learn

C. The learners' level of satisfaction with the course

D. The cost-effectiveness of the CME activity

Answer: B The extent to which learners implement what they learn

Explanation: Competence refers to the extent to which learners know how to implement or stop doing what the CME activity intended to teach them.

What is in-kind commercial support in the context of the ACCME's Standards?

A. Monetary support provided by an eligible company

B. Government grants for CME activities

C. Non-monetary support from an ineligible company for a CME activity

D. Sponsorship from non-profit organizations

Answer: C   Non-monetary support from an ineligible company for a CME activity

Explanation: In-kind commercial support includes non-monetary assistance, such as the use of equipment or supplies provided by an ineligible company for CME activities.

Question 44

What are Merit-Based Incentive Payment Systems (MIPS)?

A. A type of insurance policy for healthcare providers

B. A marketing strategy for pharmaceutical companies

C. A certification program for CME providers

D. A payment adjustment system for Medicare services based on performance

Answer: D   A payment adjustment system for Medicare services based on performance

Explanation: MIPS is a performance-based payment adjustment system under the CMS, which includes accredited CME as an Improvement Activity.

Question 45

What is the Program and Activity Reporting System (PARS)?

A. A tool for recording patient medical histories

B. A platform for patient feedback on healthcare services

C. A web-based portal for CME providers to manage activity data

D. A regulatory compliance database for hospitals

Answer: C   A web-based portal for CME providers to manage activity data

Explanation: PARS is a web-based portal designed by the ACCME for CME providers to enter, track, and manage program and activity data, as well as physician-learner information.

What is a Risk Evaluation and Mitigation Strategy (REMS)?

A. A financial risk management tool for healthcare providers

B. A safety program required by the FDA for certain medications

C. An evaluation method for CME program effectiveness

D. A strategy for marketing new medical devices

Answer: B   A safety program required by the FDA for certain medications

Explanation: REMS is a drug safety program required by the FDA for certain medications to ensure that their benefits outweigh their risks.

What is a Self-Study Report in the context of ACCME accreditation?

A. A report on patient satisfaction

B. A curriculum outline for CME courses

C. A financial report for grant funding

D. A document prepared by CME providers for accreditation purposes

Answer: D   A document prepared by CME providers for accreditation purposes

Explanation: A Self-Study Report is prepared by CME providers to explain their accomplishments, practices, and plans for improvement related to ACCME Accreditation Criteria and policies.

Question 48

What does "Accreditation with Commendation" signify in the ACCME System?

A. Initial accreditation status

B. The highest accreditation status with a six-year term

C. A temporary accreditation status

D. An optional accreditation status without a specified term

Answer: B The highest accreditation status with a six-year term

Explanation: Accreditation with Commendation is the highest status available, awarded for a six-year term to providers seeking reaccreditation.

What is AMA PRA Category 1 Credit?

A. Credit for attending unaccredited educational activities

B. A form of financial compensation for healthcare professionals

C. A type of certification for CME providers

D. The credit type earned by participating in certified CME activities

Answer: D   The credit type earned by participating in certified CME activities

Explanation: AMA PRA Category 1 Credit is earned by physicians who participate in certified CME activities sponsored by accredited CME providers.

Question 50

What is the difference between AMA PRA Category 1 Credit and AMA PRA Category 2 Credit?

A. Category 1 is for certified activities; Category 2 is self-claimed by physicians

B. Category 1 is for non-certified activities; Category 2 is certified

C. There is no difference between the two categories

D. Category 2 is only for medical students

Answer: A   Category 1 is for certified activities; Category 2 is self-claimed by physicians

Explanation: AMA PRA Category 1 Credit is for certified activities, while Category 2 Credit is self-claimed and self-documented by physicians for non-certified activities.

What does continuing professional development (CPD) include?

A. Primarily formal education activities

B. Primarily workshops and seminars

C. Primarily state-mandated training sessions

D. All activities, formal and informal, for professional growth

Answer: D All activities, formal and informal, for professional growth

Explanation: CPD includes all activities, both formal and informal, undertaken by healthcare professionals to maintain, update, and enhance their knowledge and skills.

Why is a CE Educator's Toolkit needed?

A. To promote and encourage critical thinking and collaboration

B. To provide financial resources for CME programs

C. To replace traditional lecture-based learning

D. To standardize all CME activities

Answer: A   To promote and encourage critical thinking and collaboration

Explanation: A CE Educator's Toolkit is needed to incorporate effective instructional methods that promote critical thinking, collaboration, and decision-making skills, which improve team performance and behavior change.

Question 53

What are the benefits of small group learning in CME?

A. Promotes self-esteem and participation

B. Introduces learners to a range of perspectives

C. Develops social, communication, and leadership skills

D. All of the above

Answer: D   All of the above

Explanation: Small group learning in CME promotes self-esteem and participation, introduces learners to different perspectives, and helps develop social, communication, and leadership skills.

How does case-based learning benefit CME participants?

A. Fosters critical thinking through real-world scenarios

B. Promotes collaboration and interprofessional learning

C. Uses inquiry-based approaches

D. All of the above

Answer: D All of the above

Explanation: Case-based learning benefits CME participants by fostering critical thinking, promoting collaboration, and using inquiry-based approaches to enhance learning.

Question 55

What is the purpose of reflective learning in CME?

A. To focus on memorization of facts

B. To develop self-awareness and facilitate lifelong learning

C. To encourage competitive behavior

D. To shorten the learning process

Answer: B   To develop self-awareness and facilitate lifelong learning

Explanation: Reflective learning aims to develop self-awareness, facilitate lifelong learning, and help identify individual gaps and needs.

Question 56

Which method involves directly asking learners about their perceived learning needs?

A) Expert Advisory Group

B) Focus Groups

C) Input from Patients

D) Surveys

Answer: D   Surveys

Explanation: Surveys involve directly asking learners about their perceived learning needs, providing valuable insights into their educational requirements.

Question 57

Learning objectives should clearly state what in measurable terms?

A) Learner demographics

B) The duration of the activity

C) The behavior or attitude expected after completion

D) The number of instructors

Answer: C   The behavior or attitude expected after completion

Explanation: Learning objectives should clearly state, in measurable terms, the behavior or attitude the learner is expected to adopt upon completing the activity.

What does the TACT principle stand for in making a learning objective actionable?

A) Time, Activity, Context, Target

B) Target, Action, Context, Time

C) Thought, Analysis, Context, Timing

D) Task, Activity, Content, Time

Answer: B   Target, Action, Context, Time

Explanation: The TACT principle stands for Target, Action, Context, and Time, providing a structured approach to making learning objectives actionable.

Question 59

What is an important component of program design to promote collaborative relationships in learning and clinical spaces?

A) Use of jargon

B) Inclusive and respectful language

C) Selective participation

D) Prescriptive instructions

Answer: B   Inclusive and respectful language

Explanation: Using inclusive and respectful language is an important component of program design to promote collaborative relationships in both learning and clinical spaces.

Question 60

What is an essential aspect of designing authentic learner-centered experiences?

A) Ignoring diversity

B) Focusing on uniformity

C) Paying attention to the diversity of learner needs

D) Avoiding real-life examples

Answer: C   Paying attention to the diversity of learner needs

Explanation: Designing authentic learner-centered experiences includes paying attention to the diversity of learner needs to ensure inclusivity and effectiveness.

What does designing for equity aim to address?

A) Systematic, unnecessary, unfair, and unavoidable differences

B) Elimination of diversity

C) Standardization of learning outcomes

D) Ensuring equal outcomes for all learners

Answer: A   Systematic, unnecessary, unfair, and unavoidable differences

Explanation: Designing for equity aims to address systematic, unnecessary, unfair, and avoidable differences between individuals and population groups.

How can the use of virtual platforms in learning promote accessibility?

A) By increasing cost barriers

B) By limiting reach to a larger audience

C) By reaching a larger target audience

D) By decreasing technological access

Answer: C   By reaching a larger target audience

Explanation: Virtual platforms can promote accessibility by reaching a larger target audience, facilitating broader participation in learning activities.

What is the highest level in Bloom's Taxonomy?

A) Application

B) Evaluation

C) Synthesis

D) Knowledge

Answer: B   Evaluation

Explanation: Evaluation is the highest level in Bloom's Taxonomy, involving judgment and assessment of concepts.

Which level of Bloom's Taxonomy involves problem-solving?

A) Knowledge

B) Comprehension

C) Application

D) Evaluation

Answer: C   Application

Explanation: Application involves using abstractions in concrete situations, which often entails problem-solving.

Question 65

What distinguishes small group learning from traditional instructor-led sessions?

A) Learner-driven approach

B) Instructor-centered approach

C) Passive engagement

D) Focus on individual progress

Answer: A   Learner-driven approach

Explanation: The main goal of small group learning is to have a learner-driven session, fostering active engagement and collaboration among participants.

Question 66

What is the purpose of debriefing in small group learning?

A) Introduce concepts and learning objectives

B) Foster a supportive environment

C) Prompt discussion and gauge learner progress

D) Close session and deliver knowledge assessment

Answer: D   Close session and deliver knowledge assessment

Explanation: Debriefing in small group learning involves closing the session and delivering knowledge assessments, ensuring comprehension and retention of key concepts.

Question 67

In Tuckman's stages of small group development, which stage involves resolving conflicts and establishing norms?

A) Forming

B) Storming

C) Norming

D) Performing

Answer: C   Norming

Explanation: The norming stage involves resolving conflicts and establishing norms for collaboration and interaction within the group.

Question 68

Which level of Bloom's Taxonomy involves breaking down a whole into component parts?

A) Knowledge

B) Comprehension

C) Analysis

D) Synthesis

Answer: C   Analysis

Explanation: Analysis involves breaking down a whole into component parts to understand its structure and functioning.

Which method involves obtaining information from patients' clinical records?

A) Focus Groups

B) Key Informant

C) Chart Audit

D) Expert Advisory Group

Answer: C   Chart Audit

Explanation: Chart audit involves obtaining information from patients' clinical records to identify unperceived learning needs.

Question 70

Which level of Bloom's Taxonomy involves recalling information?

A) Competence

B) Evaluation

C) Synthesis

D) Knowledge

Answer: D   Knowledge

Explanation: Knowledge involves recalling information, facts, or concepts without necessarily understanding their deeper meaning or implications.

Question 71

Which type of case involves presenting a scenario with specific learning objectives?

A) Directed Case

B) Dilemma or Decision Case

C) Interrupted Case

D) Spontaneous Case

Answer: A   Directed Case

Explanation: A directed case involves presenting a scenario with specific learning objectives, guiding learners towards predetermined outcomes.

Question 72

What is the third step in facilitating case-based learning?

A) Present the case

B) Discuss the case

C) Debrief the case

D) Analyze the case

Answer: C   Debrief the case

Explanation: Debriefing the case is the third step in facilitating case-based learning, allowing learners to reflect on their experiences and discuss key insights.

Question 73

Which of the following is NOT a common barrier to learning engagement?

A) Environmental distractions

B) Overconfidence

C) Lack of interest and motivation

D) High levels of energy

Answer: D   High levels of energy

Explanation: High levels of energy typically enhance engagement rather than hinder it.

What is one of the facilitator's roles in case-based learning discussion?

A) Introduce new distractions

B) Avoid engaging learners

C) Create safe environments

D) Limit participation

Answer: C   Create safe environments

Explanation: One of the facilitator's roles is to create safe environments where learners feel comfortable sharing their perspectives and engaging in discussions.

Question 75

What is reflective learning primarily focused on?

A) Memorization

B) Critically reflecting upon one's thoughts and actions

C) Repetition

D) Passive absorption of information

Answer: B   Critically reflecting upon one's thoughts and actions

Explanation: Reflective learning involves critically reflecting upon one's own thoughts, behaviors, and actions in various practice scenarios.

What are the stages of the Critical Reflective Inquiry (CRI) model?

A) Description, Reflection, Analysis

B) Introduction, Reflection, Critique

C) Preparatory, Review, Assessment

D) Descriptive, Reflective, Critical

Answer: D   Descriptive, Reflective, Critical

Explanation: The stages of the Critical Reflective Inquiry (CRI) model are descriptive, reflective, and critical, guiding learners through a process of deep reflection and evaluation.

Question 77

What is a common challenge associated with reflective learning?

A) Excessive time availability

B) High levels of engagement

C) Ease of assessment

D) Lack of time

Answer: D   Lack of time

Explanation: Lack of time is a common challenge associated with reflective learning, as it requires dedicated time for deep introspection and analysis.

Question 78

What is one of the key principles for facilitating reflective learning?

A) Unclear guidance

B) Impractical goals

C) Integration of concepts

D) Avoidance of deep reflection

Answer: C   Integration of concepts

Explanation: Integration of concepts is a key principle for facilitating reflective learning, ensuring that learners connect new insights with existing knowledge frameworks.

Question 79

Which framework assesses whether the CE education intervention is effective in driving current and sustained mastery and performance of professional capability?

A) RE-AIM

B) Kirkpatrick-Barr

C) Moore's framework

D) CRI model

Answer: A   RE-AIM

Explanation: The RE-AIM framework assesses whether the CE education intervention is effective in driving current and sustained mastery and performance of professional capability.

What is a method commonly used for evaluating CE sessions that involves obtaining feedback from participants?

A) Clinical vignettes

B) Simulation

C) Feedback survey

D) Learning from teaching

Answer: C   Feedback survey

Explanation: Feedback surveys are commonly used for evaluating CE sessions, providing valuable insights into participants' experiences and perceptions.

Which learning competency involves managing and administering the CE program?

A) Using Adult and Organizational Learning Principles

B) Designing Educational Interventions

C) Managing and Administering the CE Program

D) Engaging in Self-Assessment and Lifelong Learning

Answer: C   Managing and Administering the CE Program

Explanation: Managing and administering the CE program involves overseeing office operations and ensuring compliance with standards and regulations.

What does the competency "Engaging in self-assessment and lifelong learning" emphasize?

A) Compliance with regulations

B) Continuous professional development

C) Designing educational interventions

D) Managing financial operations

Answer: B   Continuous professional development

Explanation: Engaging in self-assessment and lifelong learning emphasizes the importance of continuous professional development and self-improvement.

Question 83

Which method involves using clinical scenarios to assess the application of knowledge in real-world situations?

A) Feedback survey

B) Analysis of reflective statements

C) Clinical vignettes

D) Written responses

Answer: C   Clinical vignettes

Explanation: Clinical vignettes involve using real-world scenarios to assess the application of knowledge and skills in clinical practice.

What does the competency "Collaborating and Partnering with Stakeholders" focus on?

A) Managing office operations

B) Designing educational interventions

C) Measuring the performance of CE activities

D) Establishing relationships with relevant parties

Answer: D   Establishing relationships with relevant parties

Explanation: Collaborating and partnering with stakeholders focuses on establishing and maintaining relationships with relevant parties to support the CE program's goals.

Question 85

What is a method used for evaluating CE sessions that involves learners' written responses to specific prompts or questions?

A) Feedback survey

B) Simulation

C) Written responses

D) Clinical vignettes

Answer: C   Written responses

Explanation: Written responses involve learners providing written feedback or answers to specific prompts, allowing for a more detailed assessment of their understanding and perspectives.

Question 86

Which instructional format provides educational content that can be accessed or reviewed at the learner's convenience?

a. Live activities

b. Enduring materials

c. Journal-based activities

d. Test item writing

Answer: b. Enduring materials

Explanation: Enduring materials, such as recorded lectures or online modules, provide educational content that can be accessed or reviewed by learners at their convenience, allowing for self-paced learning.

Question 87

Which instructional format typically involves reading and critically evaluating articles from published works of the professionals?

a. Live activities

b. Enduring materials

c. Journal-based activities

d. Test item writing

Answer: c. Journal-based activities

Explanation: Journal-based activities involve reading and critically evaluating articles from professional journals, helping learners stay updated on the latest research and evidence-based practices.

Which instructional format is most suitable for hands-on training and skill development?

a. Live activities

b. Enduring materials

c. Journal-based activities

d. Test item writing

Answer: a. Live activities

Explanation: Live activities, such as workshops or simulation-based training sessions, are most suitable for hands-on training and skill development, allowing learners to practice and receive immediate feedback from instructors.

Question 89

Which instructional format is most effective for self-directed learning and review of educational content?

a. Live activities

b. Enduring materials

c. Journal-based activities

d. Test item writing

Answer: b. Enduring materials

Explanation: Enduring materials, such as recorded lectures or online modules, are most effective for self-directed learning and review of educational content, allowing learners to access information at their own pace and convenience.

Question 90

Which instructional format is essential for promoting critical appraisal skills and evidence-based practice among healthcare professionals?

a. Live activities

b. Enduring materials

c. Journal-based activities

d. Test item writing

Answer: c. Journal-based activities

Explanation: Journal-based activities are essential for promoting critical appraisal skills and evidence-based practice among healthcare professionals, as they involve reading and critically evaluating research articles from professional journals.

Question 91

Which instructional format focuses on improving the quality and accuracy of assessment tools used in medical education?

a. Live activities

b. Enduring materials

c. Journal-based activities

d. Test item writing

Answer: d. Test item writing

Explanation: Test item writing focuses on improving the quality and accuracy of assessment tools used in medical education by creating well-constructed and reliable test items for evaluating learners' knowledge and understanding.

Question 92

Which of the following is a common challenge faced by healthcare professionals in their learning journey within healthcare systems?

a. Limited access to educational resources

b. Lack of interest in professional development

c. Excessive focus on administrative tasks

d. Overabundance of available learning opportunities

Answer: a. Limited access to educational resources

Explanation: Limited access to educational resources, such as time constraints, financial barriers, or lack of institutional support, is a common challenge faced by healthcare professionals in their learning journey within healthcare systems.

Question 93

Which of the following is a potential barrier to delivering optimal care in healthcare systems?

a. Language barriers

b. Cultural competence

c. Limited access to technology

d. All of these

Answer: d. All of these

Explanation: Effective communication is essential for delivering optimal care and is not considered a barrier; instead, it facilitates collaboration, patient engagement, and shared decision-making among healthcare professionals and patients.

Question 94

Which of the following is a systemic barrier to delivering optimal care in healthcare systems?

a. Patient empowerment

b. Interprofessional collaboration

c. Fragmented healthcare delivery

d. Patient-centered care

Answer: c. Fragmented healthcare delivery

Explanation: Fragmented healthcare delivery, characterized by disjointed or uncoordinated care across different providers or healthcare settings, is a systemic barrier that can hinder the delivery of optimal care within healthcare systems.

Question 95

What is the primary benefit of interprofessional collaboration within healthcare teams?

a. Increased competition

b. Improved patient outcomes

c. Reduced workload

d. Decreased job satisfaction

Answer: b. Improved patient outcomes

Explanation: Interprofessional collaboration within healthcare teams leads to improved patient outcomes by leveraging the expertise of diverse healthcare professionals to provide comprehensive, patient-centered care that addresses the complex needs of patients.

Which of the following best describes the role of the interdisciplinary team in healthcare systems?

a. Working in isolation to address patient needs

b. Focusing solely on individual professional goals

c. Collaborating to provide holistic care

d. Competing for resources and recognition

Answer: c. Collaborating to provide holistic care

Explanation: The role of the interdisciplinary team in healthcare systems involves collaborating to provide holistic care by integrating the unique perspectives, skills, and knowledge of various healthcare professionals to address the physical, emotional, and social needs of patients.

Which of the following is an external factor that can influence the availability of CPD resources?

a. Individual learning preferences

b. Institutional support

c. Government funding

d. Professional certifications

Answer: c. Government funding

Explanation: Government funding plays a crucial role in supporting the availability of CPD resources by allocating financial resources to educational institutions, professional organizations, and healthcare systems to develop and deliver CPD activities.

Which of the following external factors can contribute to changes in healthcare delivery models and, consequently, impact CPD requirements?

a. Socioeconomic factors

b. Technological innovations

c. Professional regulations

d. Individual learning preferences

Answer: b. Technological innovations

Explanation: Technological innovations in healthcare delivery models, such as telemedicine and artificial intelligence, can impact CPD requirements by necessitating training in new tools, techniques, and protocols to adapt to evolving healthcare practices and patient care needs.

Which external factor can influence the focus areas of CPD activities?

a. Personal career goals

b. Healthcare facility protocols

c. Patient demographics

d. Industry-sponsored initiatives

Answer: d. Industry-sponsored initiatives

Explanation: Industry-sponsored initiatives, such as pharmaceutical companies or medical device manufacturers, can influence the focus areas of CPD activities by sponsoring educational programs related to their products, treatments, or therapeutic areas of interest.

END OF BOOK

Made in United States
Troutdale, OR
02/07/2025